This book is revised and expanded from the previous book "Re-Tiring"

Written and Illustrated
by PAUL ~~T~~ ~~FARBER~~

The contents of this book shall not be reproduced in whole nor in part, by duplicating machine nor any other means without written permission by the author.

formerly - Tired Gardening
Re-Tired
& Re-Tiring

First Printing   Feb. 1986
First Revision   Apr. 1989
2nd Revision   Mar. 1990
3rd Revision   Mar. 1993

Copyright

© 11-MCMLXXXVI by Paul Farber

ISBN 0–916095–51–7

Introduction

A few years ago, I was fascinated with the concept of raised bed, high yield gardening, but the accepted techniques were not quite what I was looking for. Liking to change my garden layout frequently, I did not want permanent raised beds. Also, I did not relish the idea of buying a lot of boards, bricks or concrete. The more I thought about it, the more old tires seemed to be the answer. Next, the challenge was to make planters from tires, which meant cutting them. I could not find a practical tool for cutting tires, so I started experimenting.

After many unsuccessful attempts, I developed a tire cutting tool that is easy to make, inexpensive and cuts tires extremly well, enabling me to build a raised bed garden. The versatility surpassed my highest expectations.

As each tire project developed, It spawned new ones. As these new projects progressed they created interest from friends and neighbors. Because of their questions and curiosity, I decided to write this book.

I would like this book not only to show you my ideas and designs, but to stimulate your imagination to alter the projects to fit your circumstances and to create new projects.

The fun of working with tires is that you have little or nothing invested. If you get an idea, no matter how far fetched, get some tires and try it. If the project fails, discard the tire and try again. This is one of the few ways you can express your creativity, make something useful and help the environment while having fun and not spending money.

Many people and organizations are making Horse Swings, Mexican Pots and Stock Feeders for fund raisers.

I have personally tested everything in this book, and believe that all of the projects are as good or superior to their commercial counter parts, but cost a lot less. PAUL FARBER

Contents

ABOUT TIRES - chap. 1
PAGE NO.
GENERAL INFORMATION & SAFETY TIPS _____ 6
ABOUT TIRES (for our purposes) _____ 7 to 9
TOOLS FOR CUTTING TIRES _____ 10, 11
HOW TO CUT A TIRE _____ 12
TURN A TIRE INSIDE OUT _____ 13, 14
CUT HOLES IN TIRES _____ 15

MISCELLANEOUS - chap. 2
STOCK FEEDERS _____ 16 to 18
FOWL FEEDER _____ 19 to 21
FENDERS for TRAILERS _____ 22
BIRD BATHS _____ 39 & 69
POULTRY BROODER _____ 78
PERMANENT LABELS _____ 104

SWINGS - chap. 3
SWING/LIMB ATTACHER _____ 23
HOW TO MAKE SWINGS _____ 24 to 27
TIRE HORSE SWING _____ 28 to 32
SAND BOX & TREE LADDER _____ 33

RETAINING WALLS & STEPS - chap. 4
INTRODUCTION _____ 34
RETAINING WALLS _____ 35 to 37
TIRE STEPS _____ 38, 39
STEPPING STONES _____ 40, 41

SUPERIOR COMPOSTING - chap. 5

INTRODUCTION ——————————— 42, 43
HOW A COMPOSTER WORKS ——————— 44 to 46
FACTS ABOUT THE TIRE COMPOSTER ———— 48
HOW TO MAKE & USE A TIRE COMPOSTER ——— 50
METHODS OF COMPOSTING ——————— 51
CASUAL COMPOSTING ——————— 52 to 54
ACCELERATED COMPOSTING ————— 55 to 57
VERMICOMPOSTING ——————— 58 to 62

CONTAINERS - chap. 6

INTRODUCTION ——————————— 63
HOW TO MAKE A GRECIAN URN ———— 64 to 66
MEXICAN POTTERY ——————— 67, 68
POTTERY PERIMETER CUPS ————— 69
LAWN & GARDEN EDGING ————— 70, 71
STRAWBERRY PLANTER ——————— 72
HERBS ——————————— 73
ELEVATED GARDEN ————— 74, 75
COLD FRAME ——————— 76, 77
MINI GREEN HOUSE ——————— 78

SUPER INTENSIVE GARDENING - chap. 7

INTRODUCTION ——————— 79 to 81
COOL WEATHER CROP PLANTERS ———— 82
WARM WEATHER CROP PLANTERS ———— 83
GROWING MEDIUM ——————— 84
FERTILIZER ————————— 85
SOIL THERMOMETER ——————— 86
TEMPERATURE CONTROL THRU WATERING ——— 87
WATERING SYSTEMS ————— 88, 89
GARDEN LAYOUT ————— 90, 91
TOMATOES ——————— 92 to 95
VEGETABLE SUPPORTS ————— 96 to 102
POTATO PLANTER ——————— 103

GENERAL INFORMATION & SAFETY TIPS

TIRES ARE NOT DIRTY!

You get black from the road grime that is on them. When scrubbed with soap and water, tires are clean. Only from a very few old and weathered tires will the black rub off.

SCRUB ALL TIRES THOROUGHLY WITH SOAP AND WATER,

inside and out, no mater what your project, because you have no idea where they have been.

TIRES ARE NOT TOXIC

I have found **NO EVIDENCE** that anything undesirable will leach into the soil from a clean tire or steel rim.

DANGER! LEAD WEIGHTS ARE TOXIC!

REMOVE ALL BALANCE WEIGHTS FROM the RIM. This LEAD will leach into the soil and will be absorbed by the plants and YOU.

DANGER! AVOID STEEL BELT TIRES that are WORN and the BELT EXPOSED.

The wires are sharp and you could be injured.

Wear washable protective clothing and gloves while scavenging for tires.

ABOUT TIRES
(FOR OUR PURPOSES)

FIRST! it is difficult to cut through STEEL, so choose tires that don't have steel wire in the area you plan to cut.

ALL tires have wire in the bead to support and hold the tire on the rim

On the sidewall of every tire is printed a code that identifies it's common dimensions, construction and standard test. We are only interested in part of it.

Both the information and lack of information will tell us what kind of tire it is.

STEEL BELT
P215/65R15

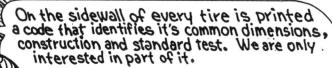

The 3 THINGS WE WANT TO KNOW

★ SIZE?

★ IS IT STEEL BELTED?

★ IS IT BIAS or RADIAL?

SIZE?

Tires are made to fit the wheel rim.

The size printed on the tire is the rim dia. and not the outside tire dia.

SOME COMMON TIRE SIZES ARE; Compact Car 13"& 14"
Full Size Car 14"& 15", Pickup Truck 15"& 16"
Semi Tractor/Trailer 20", 22.5" & 24.5" diameters.

The size we are interested in is the outside diameter and the tread width.

Use your EYE, and/or a tape measure to decide which tires you want

STEEL ?

All tires have some type of fabric or combination of fabrics throughout the tire to give it support.

These fabrics are **COTTON, RAYON, NYLON, POLYESTER, FIBERGLASS** and/or **STEEL.**

All tires have this information printed on the sidewall.

BIAS or RADIAL

If the material throughout the tire is on an angle (bias), then it is a **BIAS PLY TIRE.** If the material is square with the tire, it is a

RADIAL

MOST RADIALS are STEEL BELT
MOST BIAS are NOT

BIAS PLY

STEEL BELT

TIRE CODE

If it has an R it is a STEEL BELT RADIAL

SAMPLES ~   LT 235/75R15/C   STEEL BELT RADIAL   Rim Size

Passenger Car tire   Light Truck   STEEL BELT RADIAL   Rim Size

P165/80D13   P205/70SR14

Bias (Not an R)   Rim Size   BIAS (No R)   A78-13

8.00-15

DO N🚫T USE

RADIAL TIRES LARGER THAN 16".

THEY HAVE STEEL THROUGHOUT THE TIRE INCLUDING the SIDEWALL

WHICH TIRES DO I WANT?

STEEL BELT RADIALS—

are better for BASIC PLANTERS, SUPER INTENSIVE GARDENING, STEPS and RETAINING WALLS.

BIAS PLY TIRES—

- are essential for projects that require cutting through the tread, such as a FOWL FEEDER, LAWN & GARDEN EDGING, STEPPING STONE FORMS, STRAWBERRY PLANTER, SWINGS, SWING/LIMB ATTACHER.

- are also essential for projects that require tires larger than 16", such as for a SAND BOX or COMPOSTER.

Where can I find them?

Because almost all tires are now **STEEL BELT RADIALS,** they are plentiful at any tire service dealer.

Few **BIAS TIRES** have been manufactured in the last few years, but there are still a lot of them around. You can find them in and around garages, in vacant lots, junk yards, old tire stock piles, etc.

TOOLS for Cutting tires

You need three tools, a Drill with a 3/8" or larger Bit, a Sabre Saw with a Special Blade and a Sharp Utility Knife.

Here's how to make a
SPECIAL BLADE

Start with any New or Used woodcutting blade.

Grind to the shape of a knife with teeth

SIDE VIEW BEFORE & AFTER SHAPING

END VIEW of BLADE
BEFORE SHAPING
AFTER SHAPING

to DRESS your BLADE while you are working,

turn on saw and touch a sharpening stone to each side of the blade.
KEEP HAND BEHIND BLADE!

USE SAFETY GLASSES and LEATHER GLOVES!

WHICH SAW SHOULD I GET?

All of the tires used in the projects shown in this book, except for the Horse Swing, were cut with a domestic grade, 30 year old, Craftsman Sabre Saw.

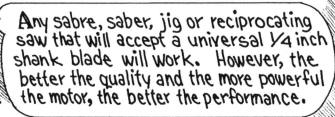

Any sabre, saber, jig or reciprocating saw that will accept a universal 1/4 inch shank blade will work. However, the better the quality and the more powerful the motor, the better the performance.

A cheap under powered jigsaw with brass bearings, cuts slower, will continually over heat and will eventually burn up.

An INDUSTRIAL rated jigsaw is more expensive, but if you plan to cut many tires, it is by far the better investment.

An ORBITAL JIGSAW is more versatile. It cuts tires faster than the standard vertical reciprocating jigsaw and will easily cut the most pliable thin sidewall.

In the past, I had to cut Horse Swings with a knife. I can now cut out the entire horse with an orbital jigsaw.

Some of the companies that make an **ORBITAL JIGSAW** are **MaKITA, BLACK & DECKER SKILL,** and **BOSCH.**

HOW TO CUT a TIRE

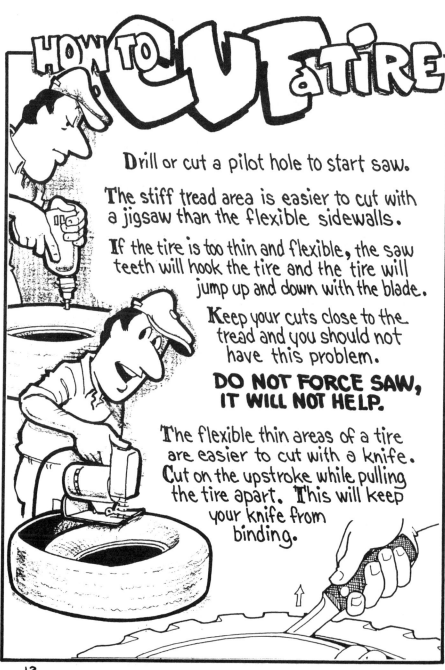

Drill or cut a pilot hole to start saw.

The stiff tread area is easier to cut with a jigsaw than the flexible sidewalls.

If the tire is too thin and flexible, the saw teeth will hook the tire and the tire will jump up and down with the blade.

Keep your cuts close to the tread and you should not have this problem.

DO NOT FORCE SAW, IT WILL NOT HELP.

The flexible thin areas of a tire are easier to cut with a knife. Cut on the upstroke while pulling the tire apart. This will keep your knife from binding.

TURN a TIRE INSIDE OUT

WITH ONLY ONE SIDE CUT OUT

BIAS TIRES, 4 ply and under, even snow tires, are much easier to turn inside out than RADIALS.

> Turning a radial inside out can be done, I do it all the time. I have also just recovered from my second hernia operation.

① cut out top close to tread.

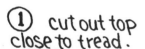

② 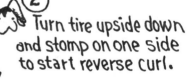 Turn tire upside down and stomp on one side to start reverse curl.

③  Stomp inside, working hands and feet, work from one point and progress around the circle.

④ It has now lost it's identity as a tire and is ready for many useful projects.

TURN a TIRE INSIDE OUT
WITH BOTH SIDES CUT OUT

Cut close to the tread on both sides.

The advantages are... You gain about two inches in height, the surface is smoother for painting, & it doesn't look like a tire.

IT'S EASY (Bias or Belt) when you learn the trick.

1 Stomp down one side.

Reach over and pull up opposite side.

2 Stretch tire up.

3

Step around tire & place other foot on opposite side.

4 Push tire over.

As you stand up, pull up the under side of the far side.

5 The tire is now turned inside out.

This works with any tire that you can stomp one side down on.

HOW TO CUT HOLES in TIRES

For STRAWBERRY PLANTERS,

GRECIAN URNS,

MEXICAN POTS ETC.

In most cases, one and a half inch diameter holes are adequate. If holes are larger, they loose soil. If smaller, they choke the plants.

Space between holes is your choice, but closer than **FOUR** inches weakens the planter.

If holes are closer than **TWO** inches from the top, the soil is likely to wash through them.

CUT HOLES BEFORE ANY OTHER CUTS

Holes are difficult to make after planter is made.

With felt marker and pattern, mark all holes but the last two.

MARK HOLE

DRILL HOLE for SAW BLADE

SAW OUT HOLE

Equally space the last two holes.

no one will notice the difference

PATTERN for HOLES
MADE FROM CARDBOARD

2" 1½" 4"

CHAP. 2- MISCELLANEOUS
StockFeeders

These are excellent, durable feeders for all your large live stock.

the GRAIN FEEDER

This feeder is not only suitable for grain and mixed feed, but it is also useful for rock salt and block salt.

How to Build

Cut the top out of one tire close to the tread and turn it inside out.

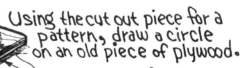

Using the cut out piece for a pattern, draw a circle on an old piece of plywood.

An inch and a half out from the first circle, free hand another circle.

1½"

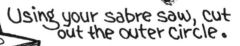

Using your sabre saw, cut out the outer circle.

Sandwich the plywood disk between the two tires

Drill four holes through both tires and bolt them together using at least 2" bolts with washers on each side.

At least 2"

the HAY FEEDER

With this feeder there is no waste because livestock cannot throw the hay out, tromp it under or foul it.

Use a tractor tire 16.9 - 24 or larger.

Cut out the bottom for good drainage and to eliminate feed loss by increasing livestock accessibility.

17

A large tire makes a good durable horse and cattle feeder, but it can easily be improved.

The problems with the tire are that the top acts as a funnel for water when it rains and the bottom collects water, encouraging rot and mildew. Under the bottom is an ideal haven for mice.

IMPROVED HORSE & CATTLE FEEDER

Cut the top out of the tire at a smaller circumference than the bottom. Reverse the bottom piece and bolt it to the top of the tire. Now the top acts as a water shed and the bottom drains to further reduce feed damage. You have also eliminated the rodent nesting area, improved the livestock accessibility and doubled the feed capacity.

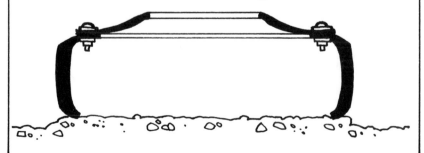

Fowl Feeder

If you need a tough, weatherproof feeder for your chickens, ducks, geese, turkeys etc. that will keep out the sheep, goats, cows, burros, horses etc., **this is it.**

This tire feeder features a lid that is animal proof, and

a canopy over the feeder holes to keep out the weather and discourage the larger animals. It is also to wobbly for goats to stand on.

How to make a FOWL FEEDER

Four non steel belt tires are required for this project. One for the canopy and latch cover, one for the base, and two for the trunk.

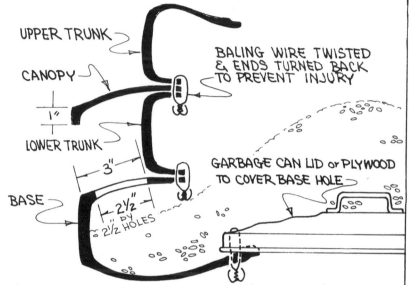

UPPER TRUNK

CANOPY

1"

LOWER TRUNK

3"

BASE

2½"
2½" BY 2½" HOLES

BALING WIRE TWISTED & ENDS TURNED BACK TO PREVENT INJURY

GARBAGE CAN LID or PLYWOOD TO COVER BASE HOLE

The canopy should be slightly larger than the base, and the base should be at least 6 inches in diameter larger than the two trunk tires.

More than 8 equally spaced 2½" x 2½" feeder holes in the base will weaken the base.

Where tires meet, diameters should be cut the same. Drill holes and wire all tires together, about eight wire ties to the level.

Stock Proof Lid for Fowl Feeder

This feeder was tested for 6 months in a children's farm exhibit at the Ogden Nature Center. This test included a burro, goat, sheep, chickens, guinea & pea fowl, geese and ducks.

After two modifications, the burro and the goat were unable to break into the feeder. After three days, all the large animals lost interest in it.

The lid is made of 1/2" CDX or thicker plywood, cut to the same circumference as the tire and painted.

Cut 6" streight end for hinge and cut 2"X4" notch for latch

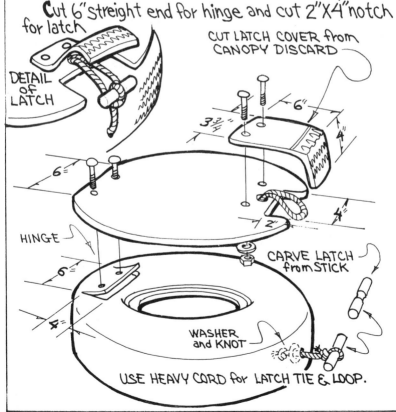

DETAIL OF LATCH

CUT LATCH COVER from CANOPY DISCARD

6"

3 3/4"

4"

6"

4"

2"

HINGE

6"

4"

CARVE LATCH from STICK

WASHER and KNOT

USE HEAVY CORD for LATCH TIE & LOOP.

FENDERS for Trailers

Consider **TIRES** if your trailer fenders need to be replaced or you are constructing a trailer that needs fenders.

They are TOUGH and FLEXIBLE and won't DENT or RUST

Because of trailer and tire variety and size, designing will have to be up to you.

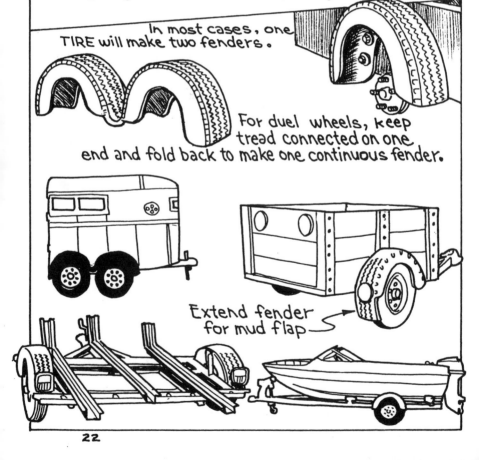

In most cases, one TIRE will make two fenders.

For duel wheels, keep tread connected on one end and fold back to make one continuous fender.

Extend fender for mud flap

Swings

There is something about a tire swing hanging from an old tree that imparts a sense of warmth and welcome.

Tire swings are so versatile that they seem to fit into practically any environment.

A child who runs into or is hit by a pliable tire swing is less apt to be injured than a child who is hit by a conventional plastic, wood or metal swing.

the SUPERDOOPER SWING LIMB ATTACHER

The most important element of any swing is how to attach it to the limb without damaging the limb or having the rope saw against itself and wear out.

Cut two belts from bias tire tread. Cut middle first.

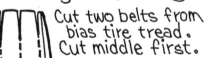

Loop SUPERDOOPER SWING LIMB ATTACHER over the limb like so.

To prevent limb damage, readjust at least once a year.

HOW TO MAKE Tire Swings

All swings should be made from non steel belted tires.

the Old Primitive

This was the swing down at the old swimming hole which was used to dive from.

It brings back a lot of fond memories, but it is very limited as a yard swing.

the BELT

Cut out a 30 inch section of bias tire tread.

Cut a one inch hole through each end, round off corners and it is ready to hang.

This is probably the best swing for one person as it is the easiest to pump.

the Old Standard

is probably the oldest design cut from a tire and it is still the best all around swing design.

The best tire for this swing is a 15" or 16" bias, well warn tire that is rounded off at the edges.

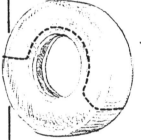

Cut out swing.

Turn swing inside out so that it is wider and more comfortable.

RIGHT SIDE OUT   INSIDE OUT

Cut a couple of holes in the bottom for water drainage.

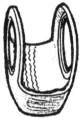

For a safe swing use at least a ½" Nylon rope

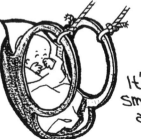

It's ideal for small children and babies

the Old Standard Improved

By extending the front edge and folding it back, the seat is flattened and becomes wider. The swing is easier to get in and out of and more comfortable on the legs.

EXTEND
FRONT EDGE

TURN SWING
INSIDE OUT

FOLD FRONT EDGE
BACK and BOLT

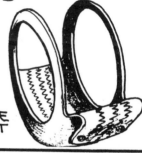

Adding a snap swivel to the rope of any swing that spins will keep the rope from winding up and wearing out.

the CRAZY SWING

This swing was developed by accident when one rope broke on the old standard.

It seems to be favored by children from four to seven years old.

It swings in all directions, spins, and has a foot rest.

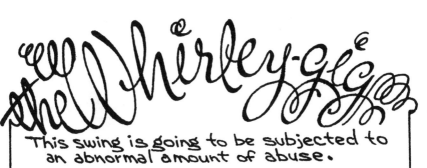

the Whirley-gig

This swing is going to be subjected to an abnormal amount of abuse.

The ropes and limb must be large enough to support a crowd of rowdy kids.

Use a 15" or 16" Bias tire for this swing.

Make first cut around bead

Second cut around tread

Cut four evenly spaced, one inch holes around tread, 1½ in. from edge

turn inside out
(if you don't, drill holes in bottom for drainage.)

Two ropes twelve feet long, folded in the middle and tied with an overhand knot.

SWIVEL SNAP

Tie the bead ring two feet from the overhand knot.

24"

24"

Tie the swing base two feet from the ring.

If you don't like a bunch of screaming, yelling, crying kids devastating the ground under your tree, don't build this swing.

The Kids love it!

28

MATERIALS

TIRE – Standard size, non steel belt, well worn with rounded edges and no threads showing.

BOLTS - 1/4" Carriage Bolts, Nuts and Washers. One 3" for mouth – One 4" for cheek / neck – One 5" for lower neck – One 8" for back – One 1 1/2" for saddle loop and tail.

LOCKTIGHT – small tube to keep nuts in place

ROPES – two each 3/8" to 5/8" dia. long enough for swing.

WASHER – one that swing rope will fit thru, but knot will not.

ROPE - small, 4 ft. long for reins.

MATERIAL – for tail (your choice).

TOOLS

TAPE MEASURE –

MARKER – black felt or tire marking crayon.

KNIFE – with large comfortable handle and short stiff blade, kept sharp.

DRILL with **3/8" BIT**   3/8"

TIN SHEARS – (optional) helps to cut through tough sections of tire.

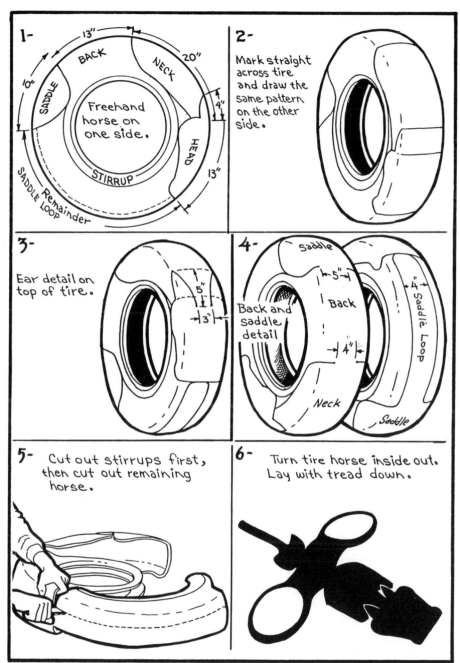

1- Freehand horse on one side.

13"
BACK
SADDLE
NECK 20"
10"
4"
HEAD
STIRRUP
13"
SADDLE LOOP
Remainder

2- Mark straight across tire and draw the same pattern on the other side.

3- Ear detail on top of tire.

5"
3"

4- Back and Saddle detail

Saddle
5"
Back
4"
4" Saddle Loop
Neck
Saddle

5- Cut out stirrups first, then cut out remaining horse.

6- Turn tire horse inside out. Lay with tread down.

30

7-

Mark and drill
all bolt holes
using 3/8" drill bit.

To attach front swing rope,
cut one inch hole, 5 inches
from ear tip and centered.

4"

Center

Center

4"

6"

2"

2"

3"

2"

1"

3"

5"

Center

8"

2"

8- Fold head and neck.
Connect with 4" bolt.

9-

Insert 3" bolt in mouth

5" bolt in lower neck

10- Detail of tail - use cord,
rags, string, baling twine
rope, etc -

11~

Attach saddle loop to
saddle with 1 1/2" bolt.

Tie swing rope to loop.

Tie tail to bolt behind
washer

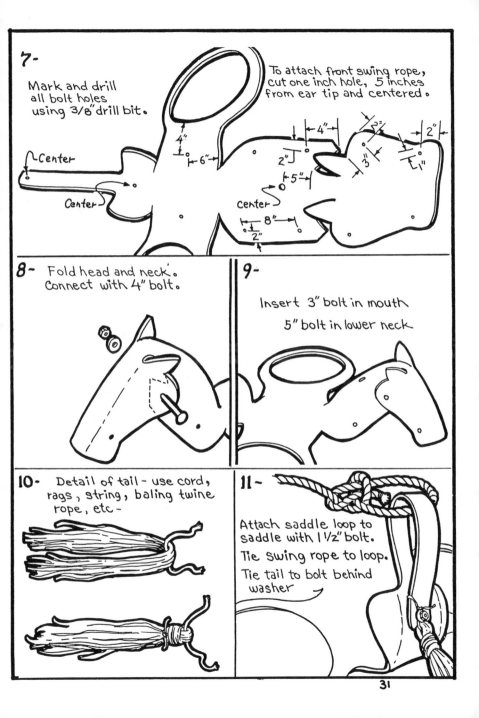

12. Put rope thru neck hole, slip washer on rope and tie knot in end of rope.

13. Hang horse. Insert 8" bolt thru back. Tie rope reins to mouth bolt.

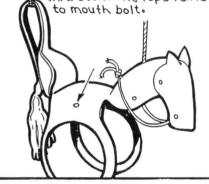

14.

Hang horse from tree limb using the Superdooper Swing Limb Attacher.

In 1985 I invented this tire horse swing for my grandchildren. They named the first two horses **Thunder** and **Lightning**.

In 1993, Thunder and Lightning are still going strong and looking as handsome as ever.

Two horses are much more fun than just one, as children love to compete. These horses will become **cow ponies, circus stallions** and **race horses** as two children out race and out perform daredevil stunts with one another. These horses will be ridden while standing in the saddle, backwards, upside down, side saddle, under the belly, and a dozen other ways that we can't think of. In fact, these horse swings get more use than all other swings combined.

TREE LADDER

Tie the tire bead rings together to form a ladder and hang it from a tree.

Sand BOX

This sand box features a safe, strong, indestructible sand container with a bench around the entire perimeter.

SEMI TRACTOR TIRE

Retaining Walls & Steps

When building steps and retaining walls in a wilderness invironment, where aesthetics are the prime consideration, seriously consider tires.

Contrary to your negative bias, tires, when properly used, are among the best possible materials. Tires, being a neutral dark gray, blend into the shadows perfectly. As a retaining wall they are actually a series of planters stacked one on the other. When planted with surrounding shrubs, vines and other ground cover, they virtually disappear.

Retaining walls and steps are resistant to the stresses of expansion and contraction and impervious to insects, ground squirrels, gophers, moles, badgers...

for STEPS, RETAINING WALLS, BRIDGE SUPPORTS, EROSION CONTROL DAMS and DIKES

Cut top out as close to tread as possible

Steel belted or non steel belted tires are O.K.

RETAINING WALLS

HILLSIDE STABILIZATION

ROAD and AQUEDUCT SUPPORTS

EROSION CONTROL

TERRACING

EROSION CONTROL

Each tire should be level and staggered like bricks.

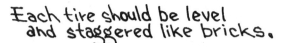

The height of each tire is more important than the radius, because the radius can be adjusted.

Sort the tires according to height

All of the tires in each row should be the same height.

Like this   Not this

Cut footing out of solid ground and level.

Fill tires with dirt, one level at a time.

FILL

EXISTING HILL

Cut footing in solid ground

If properly planted, your retaining wall should be overgrown by the second year.

USING REVERSE TIRES

ADVANTAGES -
The tires have lost their identity, you gain from 1 to 2 inches in height per tire, & by bending each tire to an oval, you use less tires per level, consequently, less tires are needed for the retaining wall.

DISADVANTAGES-
There is no bowl in the bottom of each tire for soil & moisture retention. You can not build your wall as vertical.

Use steel belt tires for rigidity. Cut both sides out as close to the tread as possible. Turn the tires inside out. Sort the tires according to height.

TO CONTROL EROSION- The hole in the bottom of each tire should not pass the center line of the two tires below it. **this determines the slant of your retaining wall.**

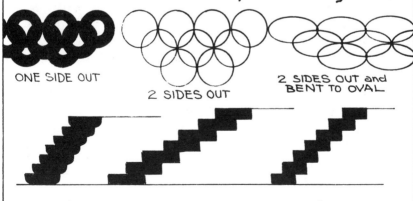

ONE SIDE OUT

2 SIDES OUT

2 SIDES OUT and BENT TO OVAL

The reverse tire retaining wall accepts latex paint beautifully.

TIRE STEPS
HOW MANY STEPS DO YOU NEED?

Each step is about seven inches high, so you will need approximately seventeen tires for every ten vertical feet.

The number of steps remain the same, no matter how steep the slope.

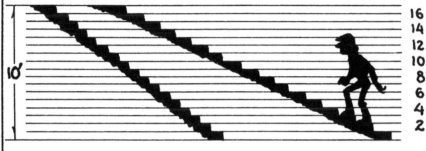

STEPS
16
14
12
10
8
6
4
2

10'

A winding stairway which utilizes the natural landscape is not only aesthetically more pleasing because it is hidden from view most of the time, but it is easier and more enjoyable to climb.

A winding stairway uses the same or fewer tires than a straight stairway.

When placing tire steps, each step must be level. Your perspective becomes distorted while you work on a hillside, so you can't rely on your eye.

YOU MUST USE A LEVEL.

Start at the bottom.

Dig a level spot large enough to set a tire.

Lay first tire into place and make sure that it is level.

Next, dig another level spot just above the first tire, using the tailings to fill the first tire.

Place second tire, level and continue as with first tire.

If soil is clay, too soft or stickey to walk on, finish off each step with rock, saw dust, wood shavings, bark, pine needles...

STEPPING STONES for Walkways

NON STEEL BELTED TIRES NECESSARY - COMPACT CAR TIRES PREFERABLE

All of these tire variations are stepping stone forms, and will need to be filled with rock, gravel or concrete.

① Simple Stepping Stones

Cut in half

Each tire makes two stepping stones.

Drill three holes in each side for drainage

Dig a trench 2 to 3 in. deep

Each tire must set level

Fill hole in center with soil

Back fill

Fill each tire with Rock or Concrete.

Printing a name and date in the wet concrete of each stepping stone gives a permanent birthday record. My grand children love to find there own and read the rest.

KATIE ANDERSON 12-15-82

JOHN ANDERSON 5-23-80

BIRD BATH

Paint light blue, surround with stones and add life to your beautiful garden.

#2
STEPPING STONES with personality

Cut the tread in three places. Make one cut down the center and two cuts as close to the sides as possible.

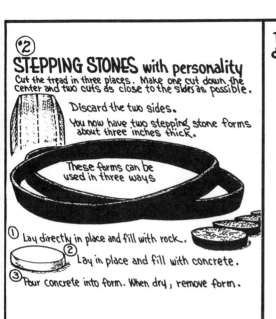

Discard the two sides.

You now have two stepping stone forms about three inches thick.

These forms can be used in three ways

① Lay directly in place and fill with rock.

② Lay in place and fill with concrete.

③ Pour concrete into form. When dry, remove form.

There are a number of designs you can make, here are a few.

LIMA   SQUARE   OBLONG

The **PEANUT FORM** – Place one form inside the other and fill inner form with concrete

PEANUT

STEPPING-STONES
How to make SQUARE forms

MATERIAL:
TWO by FOURS, 20" long – 2 ea.
TWO by TWOS, 8' long – 2 ea.
TIN, 3" X 12" – 4 ea.

DETAIL OF SLIDING CONNECTION:

Put a piece of corrugated cardboard between 2X2 and 2X4 (as shim). Wrap "TIN" around the 2X2 and tack to each side of the 2X4. Remove cardboard.

Use nails for stops, drill holes larger so nails will slip in easily.

Secure one end.

Place four tire forms into wood form.

Push and mold the tires to one end, forming squares.

Slide and force 2X4 against the tires to hold the tire squares.

Drill holes for nail stops to hold sliding 2X4 tight.

Pour concrete into forms

When concrete is dry, push stepping stones from tire forms and start over.

Chap. 5
SUPERIOR COMPOSTING

Why should we **COMPOST?**

Our nation's top soil is depleting at an alarming rate, and yet we are entombing in our already stressed landfills **OVER 25 BILLION POUNDS A YEAR** (a rate of over 100 pounds per person) of potential top soil. This packaged sunlight and energy, disguised as an apple core, potato peelings, lawn clippings etc. can be transformed back into needed top soil with minimum effort by each of us.

These are all good reasons, but I do it because it's the easiest way to get rid of my organic garbage, and it's **FUN**!

GOOD SOIL is the FOUNDATION of your GARDEN.

Improving your soil or keeping your soil in good condition is a continuing process and compost is the best all around soil conditioner you can use.

Compost retains almost 10 times it's weight of water.

Adding compost to clay soil will loosen up and aerate the soil and improve it's ability to absorb moisture.

With sandy soil, compost retains moisture which would normally drain through.

Composting also contributes needed nutrients to the soil including micro-nutrients that are not present in commercial fertilizers.

(H_3BO_3)
$(MnCl_2 \cdot 4H_2O)$
$(CuCl_2 \cdot 2H_2O)$
$(ZnSO_4 \cdot 7H_2O)$
(MoO_3)

Filling your planters with compost gives you a reason to recycle debris and a place to use the finished product.

I am having great success with straight compost in my planters for both vegetables and flowers.

HOW A COMPOSTER WORKS

A composter is like a large beast. It decomposes matter through digestion, similar to the way food is digested in the stomach of any animal.

LIKE ANY ANIMAL, IT HAS the SAME NEEDS.

FEED ME!

SEYMOUR

FOOD

To digest at its optimum, it must have a **BALANCED DIET** of **ENERGY** to **PROTEIN**

The term used is carbon to nitrogen ratio, or carbohydrates to nitrogen.

CARBON = Tough, dry, fibrous former plant parts such as autumn leaves, straw, paper, sawdust...

NITROGEN = Succulent, green vegetation and organic kitchen garbage.

25 to 30 carbon to 1 nitrogen is the ideal mix for fast composting. Grass/clover hay is 25 to 1, leaves - 50 to 1, Sawdust - 500 to 1, grass clippings - 19 to 1.

Like chewing before swallowing, the finer matter is chopped, the quicker it will digest or decompose.

IT NEEDS to BREATHE

Of the myriad organisms that decompose organic matter, by far the more important are bacteria.

There are two basic types of bacteria. **AEROBIC** (oxygen breathing) bacteria and **ANAEROBIC** (non oxygen breathing) bacteria.

As long as there is oxygen within the pile, the aerobic bacteria will swiftly decompose the materials and eliminate odors.

As soon as the supply of oxygen is exhausted, anaerobic bacteria take over, the decomposition process slows down and the compost begins to stink.

Each time you turn and aerate your compost pile, the aerobic bacteria are rejuvenated and begin their work anew.

ANAEROBIC BACTERIA

AEROBIC BACTERIA

45

IT NEEDS A DRINK

All organisms that turn wastes into humus need moisture to do their work. However, too much water will drown the oxygen breathing bacteria and the compost will stink. Ideally, the composting material should be spongy.

INTERNAL HEAT

Decomposition generates heat.

The volume of material, the energy/protein balance, oxygen and moisture determine internal temperature.

This internally generated temperature can vary from slight to as much as 180° F., depending on the method of composting.

EXTERNAL HEAT

No matter your method of composting, a warm climate enhances decomposition.

A sunny location and a solar collecting composter are ideal companions to composting, but they are not mandatory.

This is the most USER FRIENDLY COMPOSTER ever developed, it's available to everyone and it is FREE.

You will get more compost, quicker, continuously, and with less effort from this composter than from any other type of composter, pit or heap.

NO OTHER COMPOSTER OFFERS YOU ALL OF THESE ADVANTAGES

DURABILITY

This tire composter is practically indestructible and will last indefinitely.

It will not sun rot, rust, splinter, bend, warp or decay.

It will withstand the abuse inflicted by shovels, pitchforks, wheelbarrows, etc.

VERSATILITY

This composter's versatility exceeds any manufactured composter. It is suited to any requirement by simply adding or removing a unit (modified tire), or stack of units, or changing unit sizes.

It is also ideal for accelerated composting, casual composting, or vermicomposting.

SOLAR HEATED for RAPID DECOMPOSITION

The ideal temperature for composting is between 80° & 180° F.

Because the tire composter is a solar heat collector, it assists in keeping the temperature above 80° for a longer period, accelerating the decomposition process.

MOISTURE RETENTION for WORKING BACTERIA

In many composters, the heat generated through decay causes the matter to dry out, retarding decomposition and diminishing its value as a growing medium.

This composter retains moisture to enhance decomposition.

OXYGEN

Rapid decomposition requires aerating the matter. This is only achieved through frequent mixing.

This composter's unique design permits easy turning and mixing, therefore anyone can do it and do it more often.

EASY ACCESS, MIXING and REMOVAL

Quick seperation of units allows easy access to every stage of decaying matter.

This will also totally expose the humus, making it possible to remove a larger volume, easier, in less time than with other types of composters.

HOW TO MAKE and USE a COMPOSTER

Get **8** firm tires, all the same size. **4** for composting and **4** as storage. The larger they are, the more compost they will hold.

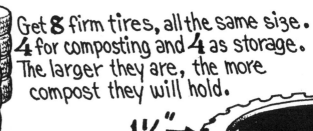

1½"→

Cut out both sides 1½ inches in from tread.

When you want a cap to keep out excess water & sun light, and keep in moisture & heat, any type cover will work. This is also a good one. See COLD FRAME for instructions.

BLACK PLASTIC

STORAGE

Choose an area about 6 ft. square, preferably in the sun, convenient to water and garden.

ALTERNATE COMPOSTER SITE

WORK AREA

1
2
3
4

6'   6'

HOW TO MIX & AERATE COMPOST

Mixing and aerating are made easy by this unique composter design.

① Pull first unit toward you, dumping contents on the ground.

② Place first unit in new location.

③ Fork contents into first unit.

④ Pull second unit off and dump contents.

Continue sequence until all units are moved to new location. Now compost is mixed and aerated.

METHODS of Composting

Advantages & Disadvantages of
CASUAL COMPOSTING, ACCELERATED COMPOSTING and VERMI-COMPOSTING

METHOD	ADVANTAGES	DISADVANTAGES
Casual Composting	Minimum maintenance. Accepts organic debris as it is created. No chopping required.	Requires maximum composting space. Up to a year for humus. Humus is not pasteurized.
Accelerated Composting	Rapid humus (2 to 3 wks.). Minimum composting space. Pasteurized humus, kills bugs, disease organisms, and weed seeds.	Labor intensive. Debris selection required. Debris must be finely chopped. Some nitrogen loss.
Vermi-Composting	Superior nutrient rich growing & potting soil. Fast humus (6 to 8 wks.). No chopping required. Little maintenance.	Will not accept large volume of matter that will heat to over 100°. Humus not pasteurized. Winter worm maintenance required.

I vermi-compost all organic kitchen garbage, summer weeds and garden refuse. Accelerated composting disposes of all lawn clippings & fall leaves. Modified casual composting takes care of the excess fall refuse.

CASUAL COMPOSTING

Casual composting is the easiest method of composting.

You simply toss all organic matter, as it is generated, into a pit or onto a heap.

Keep it moist and in approximately one year, it will become humus.

THE PROBLEMS ARE,
casual composting requires maximum composting space (approx. 39 cu. ft. per 1000 sq. ft. of yard).

Composting area is a jumble and vulnerable to scattering.

It is difficult to retrieve humus from under debris.

Do not compost meat, fat, bones, or the excrement from any meat eating animal. It is unsanitary and it stinks.

52

CASUAL COMPOSTING MODIFIED

"Casual composting in this tire composter complex makes it easy to aerate compost, keep the area neat and clean, and retrieve and store the humus.

Different organic materials decompose at different rates. However, this chart will give you an idea of 👉 the importance of mixing/aerating.

If debris is NOT decomposing within 2 weeks, it is probably lacking in protein. Add a handfull of nitrogen fertilizer and mix/aerate.

DECOMPOSITION TIME

1 YEAR

6 MON.

3 MON.

6 WKS.

0 1 2 3
TIMES AERATED

FINISHED COMPOST

As you are removing the finished compost (humus) you will probably find some undeteriorated debris such as small sticks. Pick this debris out and put it back in your composter for further decomposition.

For an excellent, uniform potting medium, screen the humus before using it.

3'
1" CHICKEN WIRE
3'

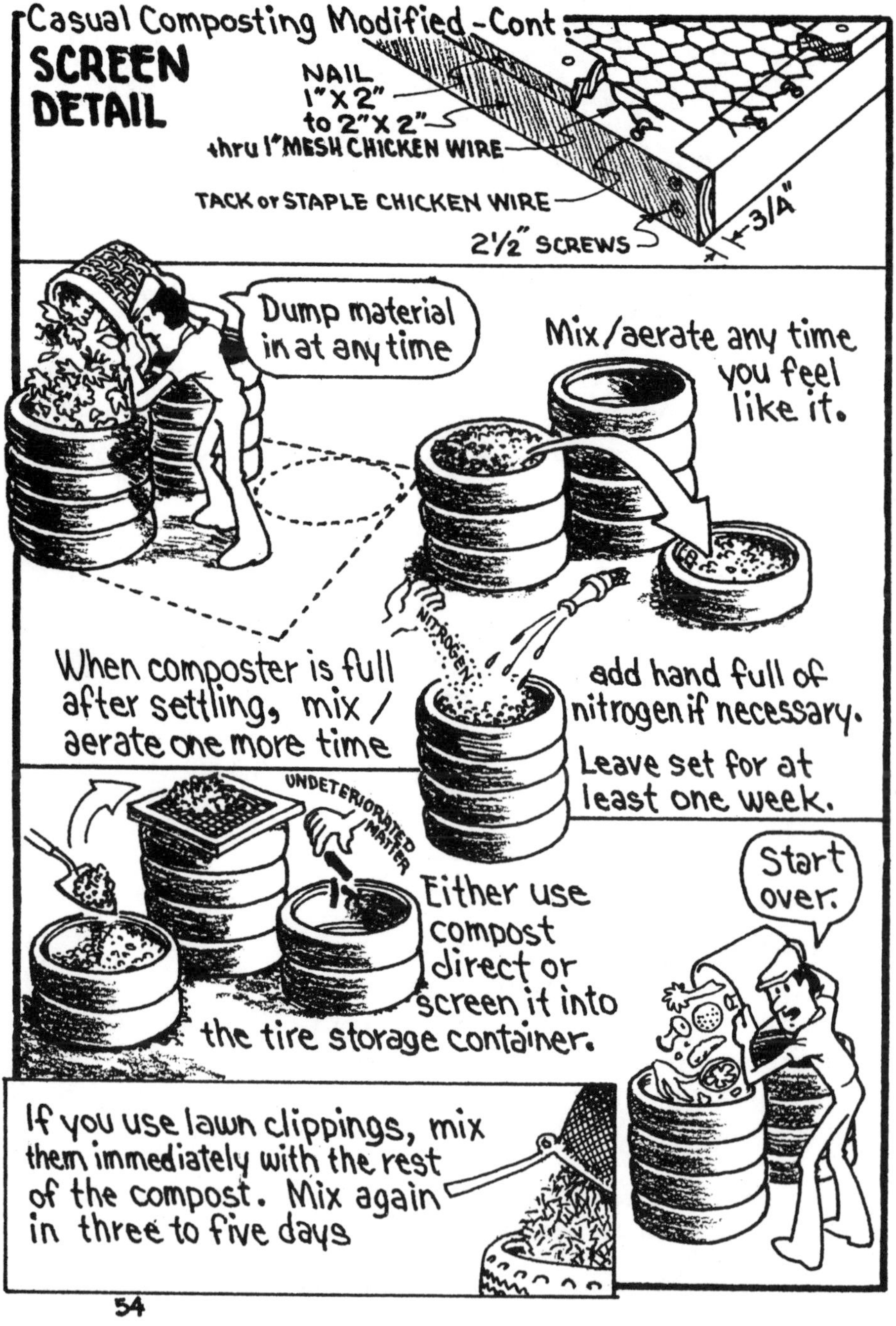

SCREEN DETAIL

NAIL 1"X 2" to 2"X 2" thru 1"MESH CHICKEN WIRE

TACK or STAPLE CHICKEN WIRE

2½" SCREWS

1 x 3/4"

Dump material in at any time

Mix/aerate any time you feel like it.

NITROGEN

When composter is full after settling, mix/aerate one more time

add hand full of nitrogen if necessary.

Leave set for at least one week.

UNDETERIORATED MATTER

Either use compost direct or screen it into the tire storage container.

Start over.

If you use lawn clippings, mix them immediately with the rest of the compost. Mix again in three to five days

ACCELERATED COMPOSTING
HUMUS in **14** DAYS

TO GET HUMUS IN 14 DAYS;

#1 the compost must generate heat from **150°** to **180°** F.

Heat is generated through mass. The heap should be at least 3 ft. by 3 ft. by 3 ft.

The outside diameter of a semi truck & trailer tire is about 3 feet, and the height of a four tire stack is about 3 feet, which make these the ideal tires for an accelerated composter.

3'

3'

#2 **EQUAL PARTS by VOLUME** (not weight) of **LEAVES** & **LAWN CLIPPINGS** are the backbone of accelerated composting. All other plant matter can be added, but the 25-30 C. to 1 N. ratio must be kept.

LEAVES

LAWN

Too much lawn and the stack will sour and stink.

Too much leaves and the stack won't work.

#3 most leaves can be composted in their natural state, but tough leaves, such as Sycamore, and all other matter must be chopped prior to composting.

#4 rapid composting quickly depletes oxygen. To replace it, you must mix/aerate the compost by the second day and every third day thereafter.

Autumn leaves and lawn clippings are not generated at the same time.

It is difficult to store lawn clippings, so the only alternative is to store leaves.

In the Fall, I put all my leaves in plastic bags.

I use them as insolation to cover fragile plants, such as rose bushes.

These bags also provide protection and easy winter access to my carrots.

Store bags until you are ready for them next summer.

DAY 1

Layer leaves and lawn clippings in the composter, alternating about every 6 inches.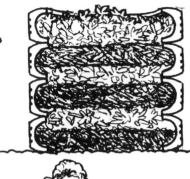

DAY 2
Mix/aerate.

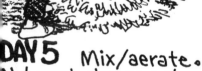

DAY 5   Mix/aerate.
Not much change yet.
Compost will reach it's' maximum
    temperature between days 5 and 8.
Mixing will become easier each time.

DAY 8
Mix/aerate. Decomposition is now obvious.

DAY 11
Mix/aerate for the last time

DAY 14
Transfer the new humus into your storage container and start over.

VERMICOMPOST

The ORGANIC GARDENER'S PLANT BOOSTER SUPREME

What is Vermicompost?

Vermicomposting is composting with the aid of worms.

Vermicompost is the castings (excrement) from earth worms.

Earth worms and their castings are odorless!

Vermicompost soil conditioner and fertilizer is among the best soil enhancers that you can use.

ADVANTAGES

You get a higher quality of growing medium, with less effort, than by any other method of composting.

You do not handle the composting material until you are ready to remove the growing medium or the worms.

Vermicompost is better textured and a more fertile planting and potting medium than any other compost.

REDWORMS

WHY REDWORMS?

Most earth worm species need a cool, established soil to survive.

The redworm prefers heat, and lives only in decaying matter. Therefore, the redworm is more suited to the composting environment.

The REDWORM (Helodrilus foetidus) is native to the eastern states, where it lives in the leaf litter of deciduous forests.

It has many other common names including manure worm, compost worm, and fish worm.

My first introduction to it was when I responded to a fishermen's magazine advertisement for "GIANT RED WRIGGLERS".

The redworm is the worm most successfully raised commercially, and is extensively cultivated and sold as fish bait.

Redworms can tolerate temperatures from 40° to 90°. However, ideal temperatures for redworm reproduction and growth are between 70° and 80°.

Redworms only eat dead material, therefore they will not harm your garden. Because redworms live only in organic matter, they will probably not survive in your garden.

SUMMARY

The redworm's tolerance for heat, it's voracious appetite, it's rapid reproduction and the extraordinary plant booster that it leaves behind, make the redworm an ideal addition to your composter.

WHERE CAN I GET REDWORMS?

★ Bait shop ★ Fishing supplies catalog ★ Fishermen's magazine ad. ★ Seed and garden supply catalog ★ Nursery & garden supply store ★ Gardening magazine ad.

HOW MANY REDWORMS DO I NEED?

2 lbs. are ideal. 1/2 lb. will multiply to over two pounds through the summer.

CARING FOR REDWORMS

FEED - Redworms have a ravenous appetite. You must continuously add new matter. Allowing the composter to lie dormant will force redworms to leave or starve.

Redworms will eat about anything, such as weeds, leaves, lawn clippings, garden debris, fruit, vegetables, table scraps including pastries, and egg shells.

To PREVENT DISEASE, don't use excrement from any meat eating animal. Also don't use meat or fat.

DO NOT FEED a large volume of matter that will heat up to over 100°.

WATER - The compost must be kept damp, too wet and the redworms will drown.

NO SAND - Although adding sand to vermicompost improves it's quality as a potting medium, do not put sand in composter. It could kill your redworms.

OXYGEN- Only the top three inches of vermicompost (below the debris) is active, and the rest is semi-dormant. Although redworms need to breathe, most of them are close to the surface and get adequate ventilation from the top.

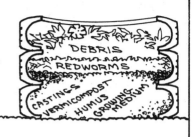

In fact, redworms do much better if they are not disturbed. It is also easier to separate humus, worms, and debris, if they are not mixed.

PROTECT FROM FREEZING. Redworms and their eggs will die if frozen.

HOW to INSULATE REDWORMS for WINTER

COVER

KITCHEN SCRAPS

Dry Leaves

Red-worms

Variety of rich organic material

1'to 2' PIT

① Dig a pit 1 to 2 ft. deep. Place one tire 1/2 under ground. Bank it with dirt to keep out water.

② Fill pit and tire with a variety of rich organic material. Make a large pocket in the middle.

③ Place redworms (1st 3" of previous vermicompost) in the pocket.

④ Add three more tires and 3/4 fill with dry leaves. Cover to keep out moisture.

⑤ Continue using composter throughout the winter to dispose of kitchen scraps.

REMOVING VERMICOMPOST and
SEPERATING VERMICOMPOST, REDWORMS and DEBRIS

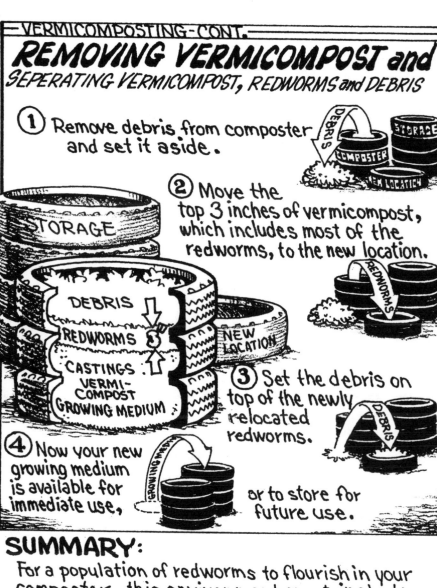

1. Remove debris from composter and set it aside.

STORAGE
COMPOSTER
NEW LOCATION

2. Move the top 3 inches of vermicompost, which includes most of the redworms, to the new location.

STORAGE

DEBRIS
REDWORMS
CASTINGS
VERMI-COMPOST
GROWING MEDIUM

NEW LOCATION

REDWORMS

3. Set the debris on top of the newly relocated redworms.

DEBRIS

4. Now your new growing medium is available for immediate use,

GROWING MEDIUM

or to store for future use.

SUMMARY:

For a population of redworms to flourish in your composter, this environment must include

★ a continuous supply of organic matter
★ moisture ★ oxygen ★ protection from killing frosts.

CHAP. 6
ATTRACTIVE, INDESTRUCTIBLE
CONTAINERS
from USED TIRES

Here is the opportunity to create gardens where plants don't ordinarily flourish. With these containers, balconies and patios sparkle with colorful blooms and over flow with edible produce.

These containers make the FUN of GARDENING available to EVERYONE!

SELECTING PLANT VARIETIES

Select those varieties that help you get the most out of available container space. Grow plants closer together than you would normally in the garden.

VEGETABLES- Select high yielding varieties of beans, beets, carrots, lettuce, peppers, radishes, and compact varieties of squash and tomatoes.

FLOWERS -Select varieties that grow well in the space and environment available. Some of the easier to grow, annual varieties are - Alyssum, Candytuft, Coleus, Impatiens, Lobelia, Marigolds, Nasturtium, Petunia, Phlox, Portulaca & Zinnia.

HERBS-Almost all varieties are ideally suited to these containers.

HOW TO MAKE a Grecian Urn

When completed, these containers resemble urns sculptured from stone or clay and require close scrutiny to determine their true identity.

① Steel belt is an option, but it is much more difficult to turn inside out.

The tire for this project should have its rim securely in place.

The tire can be well worn, but should not have any cut or tear, except in the area to be discarded.

Damage in area to be discarded

② Most tires have lines molded in the sidewalls which are ideal guides to follow while cutting.

1st cut - 1 to 2 inches from rim.

2nd cut - just in from the tread

③ OPTIONAL

Acquire a large friend.

What's a Grecian Urn?

About five bucks an hour.

4 Lay tire cut side down.
One person stand inside on rim, the other on the outside.

Reach under and lift up, turning inside out.

Using hands and feet, start at one point, pulling up and molding. After one side is up, work around the tire.

It's worth the challange!

5

Clean all the rust from the rim.

6 Scrub with soap and water. Rince and dry thoroughly.

65

(7) Paint the urn, including the first three inches of the inside with two coats of **LATEX EXTERIOR** paint.

(8) Put urn into place.

Lay a piece of plastic in the bottom to hold the growing medium and water.

Add the growing medium to your urn.

Design and layout is limited only by your imagination.

Tire with both sides cut out & turned inside out

Inside out planter setting on cut out piece.

MEXICAN POTTERY

Every Pot is unique

Each has its own shape,
and there is a different
and beautiful pattern
inside every tire that
is transferred to the
outside of the pot.

HOW TO MAKE A MEXICAN POT

Start with a tire planter. Painting it with multiple earth colors gives it the illusion of a Mexican clay pot.

Use quality latex outside flat, semigloss, or gloss paint.

This is just one easy way to paint your pot.

Start with 2 cans of paint. One dark, such as dark brown or earth red and the other light, such as light tan or yellow ochre

Paint top outside rim and inside first three inches plus the base, stem and bottom half of bole with first color. (either dark or light)

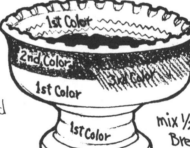

1st Color
2nd Color
3rd Color
1st Color
1st Color

Second color- Paint top half of bowl.

For 3rd Color mix ½ dark & ½ light. Break up mid bowl line with crude 45° angle strokes.

HOW TO MOUNT POT on PLANTER BASE

Center wheel inside planter base, fill with potting soil and plant.

Now place pot on wheel, insert plastic, add potting soil and plant.

POT for SUCCULENTS

Pottery Perimeter Cups

The cups work better than just holes in the side of a planter because they reduce erosion and water loss. The side plants do better and they are held up for a more beautiful display.

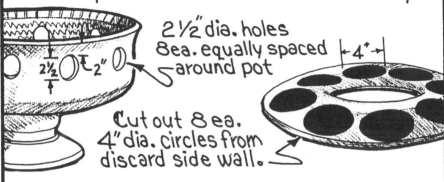

2½" dia. holes
8 ea. equally spaced
around pot

├─4"─┤

Cut out 8 ea.
4" dia. circles from
discard side wall.

Fold 4" circle and
place it in the hole.

BIRD BATH

Set garbage can lid on soil in center of pot and plant short foliage around it.

Lawn and Garden EDGING

This edging is superior in every way, and just as attractive as any commercial edging you can buy.

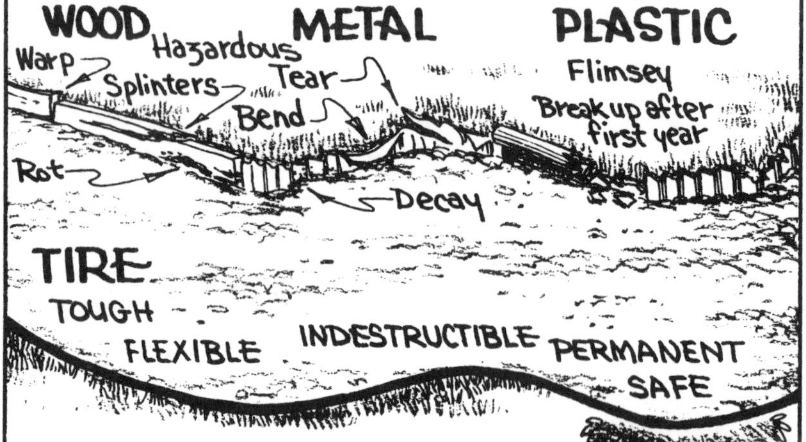

WOOD — Hazardous
Warp
Splinters
Rot

METAL
Tear
Bend
Decay

PLASTIC
Flimsey
Break up after first year

TIRE
TOUGH
FLEXIBLE   INDESTRUCTIBLE   PERMANENT
SAFE

Tire edging is safe from slivers, cuts and scratches. It's lawn mower safe and easy on the line of my fishline trimmer.

A young tree in your lawn is an ideal place for TIRE EDGING.

The edging holds in moisture and mulch while keeping the lawn mower & trimmer away from the tender bark.

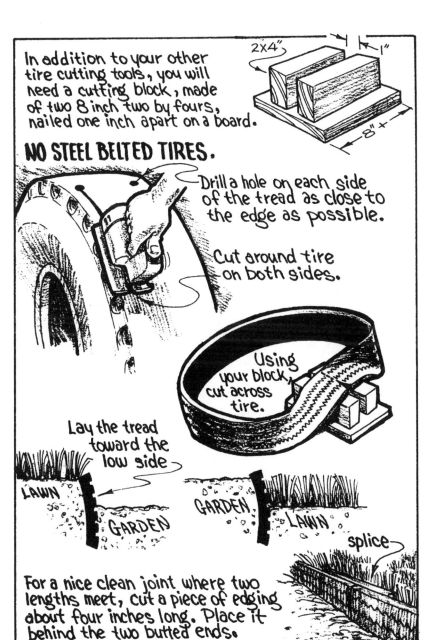

In addition to your other tire cutting tools, you will need a cutting block, made of two 8 inch two by fours, nailed one inch apart on a board.

2x4"

1"

8"+

NO STEEL BELTED TIRES.

Drill a hole on each side of the tread as close to the edge as possible.

Cut around tire on both sides.

Using your block, cut across tire.

Lay the tread toward the low side

LAWN

GARDEN

GARDEN

LAWN

splice

For a nice clean joint where two lengths meet, cut a piece of edging about four inches long. Place it behind the two butted ends.

the STRAWBERRY PLANTER

Get three different size non steel belted tires. Cut all holes, and then cut out both ends of each tire.

Turn planters inside out.

Paint with white or pastel latex exterior paint.

Do this on all three tires

Put largest planter into place. Add growing medium up to the holes.

Put plants through holes, laying roots on growing medium.

Finish filling the planter with growing medium.

Center second and third planters, following the same procedure as the first.

Now plant all flat areas.

Strawberries do best on the east, west and top of the planter. The south side is too hot and the north side is too shady. Use this to advantage by accenting your planter with flowers.

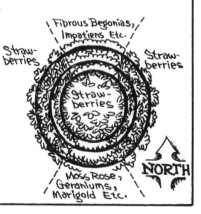

Fibrous Begonias, Impatiens Etc.

Straw-berries

Straw-berries

Straw-berries

NORTH

Moss Rose, Geraniums, Marigold Etc.

HERBS

There is a special romance with herbs in the kitchen which contribute greatly to the quality of family living.

To not only be able to enjoy their taste and smell, but also their form and beauty in an attractive setting near your kitchen door would be most enjoyable.

These multipurpose plants lend themselves beautifully to your containers.

ELEVATED GARDEN
48 sq.ft. of garden on 1 sq.ft. of lawn.

A few years ago, a neighbor's trees took over my vegetable garden so I made a new garden in a sunny location on my lawn. Using a broken telephone pole, 8 cross arms and 16 tire pots, I was able to gain approximately 48 square ft. of garden space on about one square foot of lawn.

And now my dog can't lay or dig in the garden.

Elevated Garden Stand
How to Build a 5 Planter Stand

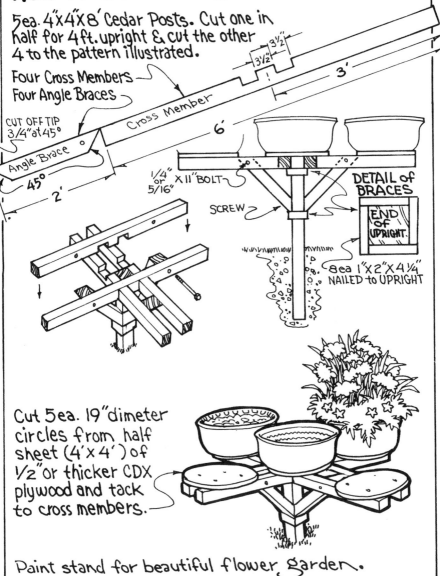

5ea. 4"x4"x8' Cedar Posts. Cut one in half for 4ft. upright & cut the other 4 to the pattern illustrated.

Four Cross Members

Four Angle Braces

CUT OFF TIP 3/4" at 45°

Cross Member

Angle Brace

45°

2'

3½" 3½"
3½"

3'

6'

1/4" or 5/16" X 11" BOLT

SCREW

DETAIL of BRACES

END OF UPRIGHT.

8ea 1"x2"x4¼" NAILED to UPRIGHT

Cut 5ea. 19"dimeter circles from half sheet (4'x4') of ½"or thicker CDX plywood and tack to cross members.

Paint stand for beautiful flower garden.

How to make a COLD FRAME

Choose a tire without a steel belt

Cut close to bead
and discard.

Cut close to tread
and save.

Turn inside out.
Paint inside with
white Latex paint.

Do not paint outside

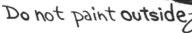

Turn upside down.

Lay clear plastic
over hole.

set ring on plastic.

How to USE YOUR COLD FRAME

Nurseries don't always have the variety of vegetable plants that you want at the time you want them. Also, flats of flower and vegetable plants are more expensive than starting your own seeds.

There is also the satisfaction of starting your own plants.

SUNLIGHT and HEAT

HEAT ABSORPTION

LIGHT and HEAT REFLECTED

Truck Tire

Growing Medium.

Drain hole

Either start your seed flats in the house, then transplant to pots and move them to the cold frame, or plant seeds directly to cold frame.

On nice days, remove plastic to circulate air and reduce heat. In evening replace plastic to conserve heat.

NO OTHER COLD FRAME is as VERSATILE

Use on raised bed or directly on the ground.

You can move the plants to the COLD FRAME or take the COLD FRAME to the plants.

Use for HOT CAPS, HARDENING OFF PLANTS, STARTING SEEDS & CUTTINGS, FORCING BULBS, EXCELERATING STRAWBERRIES.

It makes an ideal COVER for your COMPOST STACK.

MINI GREEN HOUSE

Bolt a light fixture in a tire cold frame, and you have a MINI GREEN HOUSE.

An Ideal green house to start all your household vegetables and flowers.
It is also —
Crop protection against an unexpected frost.

40 W

Poultry Brooder

Bolt a light fixture in a tire COLD FRAME and you have a POULTRY BROODER.

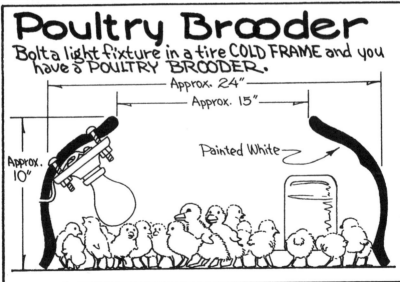

Approx. 24"

Approx. 15"

Approx. 10"

Painted White

SUPER INTENSIVE gardening

is harvesting a **MAXIMUM YIELD,**
in **LESS TIME,** in **LESS SPACE,**
and with **LESS EFFORT**
with
**SOLAR, RAISED BED, VERTICAL,
HIGH YIELD, HOME GARDENING.**

This is achieved by;
1. Versatile, solar, raised bed containers.
2. Light, loose, moisture retaining humus.
3. Ideal temperatures.
4. Adequate sun light.
5. The right seed or plant.
6. Proper planting & care techniques.
7. Correct watering.
8. Correct fertilizer & fertilization.

This chapter will address all of these subjects.

facts about Solar, Raised Bed, Vertical, High Yield, Home Gardening with TIRE CONTAINERS

VERTICAL GARDENING

achieves a high yield in a small area, crops are handy and visible. You bend over less to tend and harvest. There is even crop maturity, no ground rot and pests are more visible, therefore easier to control.

RAISED BEDS

are containers that hold the growing medium. They keep the garden level, eliminating erosion while providing good drainage. The garden is defined and attractive. Paths are clean and accessible.

TIRE CONTAINERS

use less water, are indestructible and more versatile in small, uneven or irregular plots. They can be designed for warm weather crops, collecting heat from the sun, accelerating germination, plant growth, and harvest time, or to repel heat for cool weather crops. They can be made attractive for porch and patio. They are easy and fun to make from tires that are free, available, easy to handle and transport.

No other raised bed forming material is as versatile as Tire Containers

I would like to state here that all the information I give about COMPOST, GROWING MEDIUM and FERTILIZER is from personal experience, gleaned from trial and error, books, pamphlets, soil tests from the Utah State University, and from talking to friends and neighbors with similar experiences.

Your experience and environment may or may not be similar.

There are numerous books on these subjects. Your local county extension agent or the nearest university will be glad to assist you.

HOW TO BUILD BASIC PLANTERS

There are TWO types of basic planters. Planters for COOL weather crops and Planters for WARM weather crops.

for COOL WEATHER CROPS

Such as lettuce, Spinach, peas, carrots, cabbage etc. Cut the tire as close to the tread as possible, to minimize heat absorption.

Cut out both sides of tire for good drainage and to keep soil aerated and cool.

PAINT the tire with any White or light colored LATEX paint to reflect the SUN.

EXTERIOR LATEX PAINT

TIRE PAINTED WHITE

Growing Medium

Growing Medium

Soil for high yield gardening should stay loose, airy, and retain water, to allow roots to spread with minimum effort.

The last few years, I have filled my containers with **4/5** compost & **1/5** sand, with great crop success.

Previously, I used the mix described below. I found it just as productive but it takes more effort to obtain.

1/2 peat moss or **saw dust, 1/4 compost** (home made) and **1/4 sand** all thoroughly mixed.

SAW DUST or PEAT MOSS   COMPOST   SAND

5   5 gals   +   5 gals   +   5 gals   =

APPROXIMATELY ONE TIRE FULL

about 2.8 cu. ft.

Saw dust will draw nitrogen from the surrounding soil and rob it from the plants.

If using saw dust, add 1/2 cup **AMONIUM SULFATE 21-0-0** to feed the saw dust.

If using peat moss, add 1 cup **LIME** to sweeten the peat moss.

FERTILIZER

Although compost is rich in nutrients, and has many micro nutrients that plants need but are lacking in commercial fertilizers, it does not contain the volume of major nutrients Super Intensive Gardening requires.

Container gardening depletes the nutrients so rapidly that it is difficult to replace them with organic fertilizers. Also you might not have access to organic fertilizer.

A balanced fertilizer should be mixed into the growing medium prior to planting. Suplemental feeding should continue at least twice a month throughout the growing season.

This one works well for me.

For 15" or 16" tire planter, filled with 4/5 compost & 1/5 sand.

PRIOR TO PLANTING - PER TIRE - thoroughly mix in

16/16/16 or **16/16/8** – 1/2 CUP

GYPSUM – ONE CUP

MAGNESIUM SULFATE (EPSOM SALT) - 1 HEAP TBL. SP.

EVERY OTHER SATURDAY THEREAFTER

16/16/16 or **16/16/8** - Stir 1 heaping table spoon in 5 gal. container of water.

Pour 1 gallon in each of 5 planters prior to watering, then finish watering.

A SOIL
THERMOMETER
is a must

You will achieve greater gardening success by planting when the soil is at the ideal temperature than you will by relying solely on the proper season or recommended date.

The seed from every species of plant must reach it's proper temperature to germinate, and each plant will only grow within it's particular temperature bounds. Cold soil is just not ready to support certain plant life. The necessary nutrients for plants are converted from organic matter by micro-organisms that are not active in cooler temperatures.

COLD WEATHER CROPS

Beets, broccoli, cabbage, carrots, cauliflower, celery, Chinese cabbage, kale, leeks, lettuce, onions, parsley, peas, radishes, spinach and Swiss chard all grow well when planted at **50°F.**, but if you get "antsy" and need to plant earlier, peas will germinate at **40°** and Swiss chard will start when the soil is just above freezing. Most of these plants will not tolerate soil temps. above **85°**.

WARM WEATHER CROPS

Wait untill the soil is at least **60°** before sowing beans, corn, cucumbers, eggplant, melons, peppers, squash & tomatoes.

Maximum gardening success not only depends on soil temperature monitoring, but soil temperature control as well.

TEMPERATURE CONTROL through WATERING

WATERING LOWERS the SOIL TEMPERATURE.

COLD WEATHER CROPS

Daytime watering promotes evaporation (refrigeration), reducing soil temperature.

To keep the soil temperature at a minimum for cold weather crops, water during the early afternoon.

WARM WEATHER CROPS

The roots of warm weather crops love heat. As long as the soil temperature is above 60°, these plants will continue to grow, even during the night. As soon as the soil temperature drops below 60° the plants stop growing.

Watering during the day or evening will impede warm weather crop growth. Water these plants early in the morning when the soil is already cool.

Watering Systems

There are endless ways to water a garden, and there are many good systems on the market. Most of them expensive.

1 Here are two systems I like.

Wick Watering System

If you are going to be away for a few days, this is an excellent system. Be sure to test it before you leave. A slight variation in wick size can mean a substantial difference in water volume to the plants.

DETAIL

5gal. Jug
WATER

WICK

WIRE HOOK TO HOLD WICK UNDER the SOIL

YOU NEED -

A 5gal. jug or bucket with lid.

Cotton is the best wick material. heavy cotton string or narrow strips of towel work well.

You can also add liquid fertilizer to the water

② PVC Watering System

I like this system because it is inexpensive, easy to make, easy to install, and all of the pieces separate for easy storage or to change your garden layout.

Lay out garden pattern, with tires, to measure pipe lengths, then move tires and install the system. Replace tires & fill.

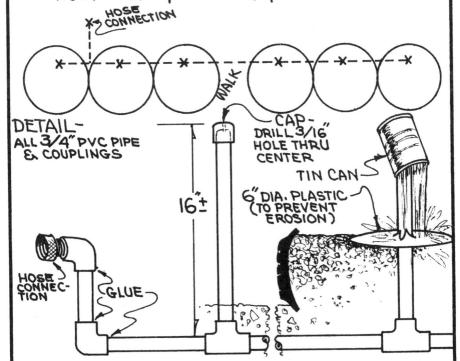

HOSE CONNECTION

WALK

DETAIL -
ALL 3/4" PVC PIPE & COUPLINGS

CAP - DRILL 3/16" HOLE THRU CENTER

TIN CAN

16±

6" DIA. PLASTIC (TO PREVENT EROSION)

HOSE CONNECTION

GLUE

GLUE ONLY THE COUPLINGS CLOSE TO THE HOSE CONNECTION. ALL OTHERS, PRESS FIT FOR EASY DISASSEMBLE, STORAGE AND RELOCATION.

GARDEN LAYOUT

It is important that each tire be level and

That each crop gets adequate sunlight.

If you are planning a vertical garden with multiple tire supports, or in order to use an automatic or mechanical watering system, it will be easier to lay your tires in rows.

The rows should run NORTH and SOUTH so all plants receive sunlight.

VEGETABLES

The following is a partial list of crops which grow well from seed in your tire planters. Included is the recommended amount of rows and the space between the plants in a row.

NAME of VEGETABLE	DISTANCE BETWEEN SEEDS	No. of ROWS
BEAN (bush)	3"	2
BEET *	2"	3
BROCCOLI	14"	1
CABBAGE	14"	1
CARROT *	1/2"	3
CAULIFLOWER	14"	1
CHARD	10"	1
CUCUMBER	14"	1
EGGPLANT	14"	1
ENDIVE *	10"	2
KOHLRABI *	3"	3
LETTUCE (head)	14"	1
LETTUCE (leaf) *	2" to 4"	3
ONION *	2	3
PEANUT	3" to 4"	2
PEPPER	10"	1
RADISH *	close"	3
SPINACH *	3"	3
TURNIP *	3"	3

* two or more crops a year.

1 Row
2 Rows
3 Rows
4"
5"
2"
3"
3"
3"

For small seeds, it's a good idea to cover the planted planters with burlap or cheese cloth until seeds sprout. Keep soil damp by watering through the cover. Remove cover immediately after first sign of sprouting.

How to Plant vertical High Yield TOMATOES

The tomatoes must be of the **Indeterminate** varieties.

Plant tomato **horizontally** and turn up end.

The sun will warm the earth around the original roots, encouraging immediate growth.

New roots will sprout along the stem, adding to its strength and vigor.

HOW TO PRUNE a TOMATO PLANT to ONE STEM

pinch all suckers off even if they have blossoms or fruit

Suckers grow in the leaf stem crotch.

Fruit grows on the stem between leaves

remove sucker

Cut off all leaves that are below the fruit

Cut off leaves that touch the ground.

Vertical High Yield TOMATOES
MULTIPLE TIRE SUPPORTS

Start with WARM WEATHER PLANTERS

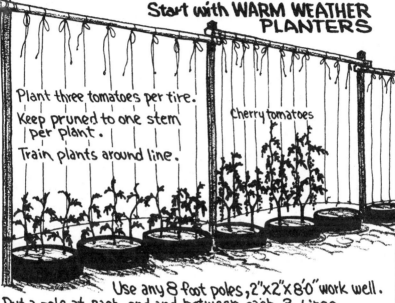

Plant three tomatoes per tire.

Keep pruned to one stem per plant.

Train plants around line.

Cherry tomatoes

Use any 8 foot poles, 2"x2"x8'0" work well. Put a pole at each end and between each 3 tires. Bury poles about 16 in. deep. Tie cross arms to uprights.

Use heavy twine for this project. (I use baling twine from a local dairy.)

Tie a line across the bottom. Next, tie three 8ft. long, evenly spaced lines, over each tire. Tie with a knot at the bottom and a bow at the top.

For cherry tomatoes – plant two per tire, with Two lines per plant. Develop two main stems per plant.

Cherry tomatoes are so vigorous, that with one stem they will outgrow the support.

Vertical High Yield TOMATOES
SINGLE TIRE SUPPORT

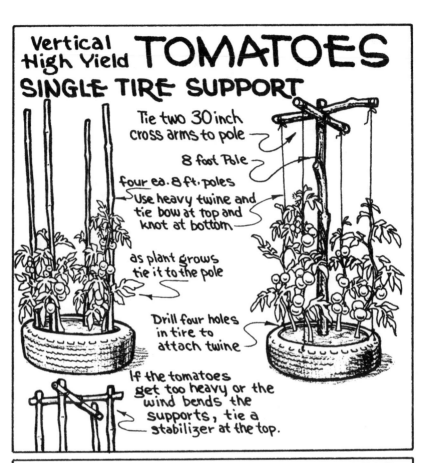

Tie two 30 inch cross arms to pole

8 foot Pole

four ea. 8 ft. poles

Use heavy twine and tie bow at top and knot at bottom

as plant grows tie it to the pole

Drill four holes in tire to attach twine

If the tomatoes get too heavy or the wind bends the supports, tie a stabilizer at the top.

There are two main varieties of tomatoes, the **INDETERMINATE** and the **DETERMINATE**. Each of these varieties serve a special purpose in your tire planters.

INDETERMINATE tomatoes grow continuously with vigorous vine growth developing fruit throughout the growing season. The plants should be staked, pruned and the fruit thinned for best results.

DETERMINATE tomatoes are self topping and do not require staking. They grow from 3 to 5 feet high and stop. The energy then goes into developing fruit. All the fruit matures at about the same time.

94

Determinate TOMATOES

Determinate tomato plants are beautifully thick and compact, with dark green leaves and bright red fruit. They are as well suited to your flower garden as to your vegetable garden.

Trimming should be kept to a minimum as it will reduce the fruit yield.

All the fruit matures at about the same time, which is an advantage in canning.

Staking is unnecessary, but caging is often used.

NOTE- keep all dead matter cleaned from under your plants. Pick off all yellow and dead leaves.

These tomato plants and flowers make a beautiful combination for your planters.

DISADVANTAGES...
All the fruit matures at about the same time and then the plant dies. Being compact, ripe fruit is often hidden and overlooked. It is also more difficult to control pests.

Growing **DETERMINATE TOMATOES** is well worth the minor inconvenience.

POLE BEAN SUPPORTS
Multiple Tire Supports
Start with warm weather crop planters

3" to 4"

All poles 8' long, tied together with string

Lace string between the two horizontal poles, spacing every three or four inches.

Make two straight rows, six inches apart in planters.
Plant beans two inches apart in the rows.

SINGLE TIRE SUPPORTS

These supports are the same as the vertical tomato supports.

Plant 6 to 8 beans to the pole or string.

CUCUMBER, MELON & SQUASH-
NET SUPPORT

Although being functional & attractive, this support looks difficult to make.

But in fact, it is quite easy.

① Make frame from 8 ft. material

With a felt marker, make a mark every 6 in. along the horizontal bar

Heavy Cord or wire

Warm weather crop planters

6'-6"

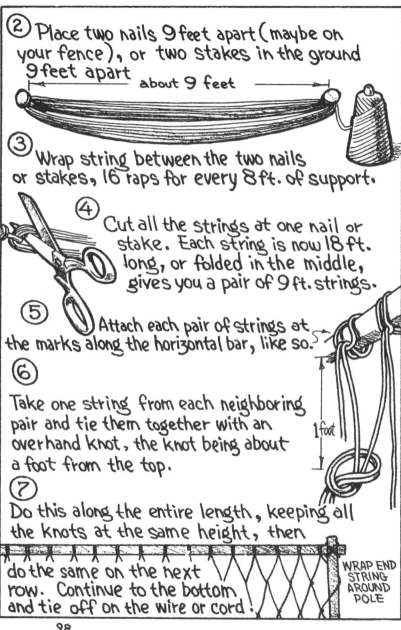

② Place two nails 9 feet apart (maybe on your fence), or two stakes in the ground 9 feet apart

about 9 feet

③ Wrap string between the two nails or stakes, 16 raps for every 8ft. of support.

④ Cut all the strings at one nail or stake. Each string is now 18 ft. long, or folded in the middle, gives you a pair of 9 ft. strings.

⑤ Attach each pair of strings at the marks along the horizontal bar, like so.

1 foot

⑥ Take one string from each neighboring pair and tie them together with an overhand knot, the knot being about a foot from the top.

⑦ Do this along the entire length, keeping all the knots at the same height, then do the same on the next row. Continue to the bottom and tie off on the wire or cord!

WRAP END STRING AROUND POLE

CUCUMBERS

For best root separation, stagger three plants to the tire, along the support

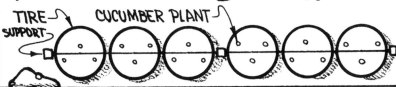

TIRE
SUPPORT
CUCUMBER PLANT

Cucumbers need more water, and almost twice the amount of fertilizer as most other plants.

12-12-12

You might like to try this layout.

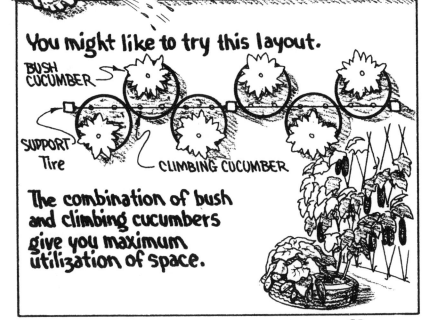

BUSH CUCUMBER

SUPPORT Tire

CLIMBING CUCUMBER

The combination of bush and climbing cucumbers give you maximum utilization of space.

SQUASH, MELON & CANTALOUPE

The same layout for cucumbers applies to squash and melons.

There are so many varieties of squash and melons that you will have to know the variety in order to determine the number of plants per tire.

MELON BAGS

Some squash, melons and cantaloupe are too heavy for the vines, and will break them down. In order to prevent this, make a bag for each fruit. Be sure to allow for growth.

Tie strings to the corners of a rag, piece of burlap or onion sack.

Or make your own ⇒

MELON TENT just for fun

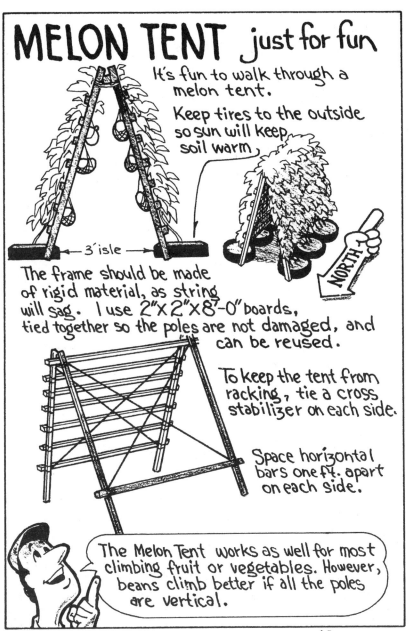

It's fun to walk through a melon tent.

Keep tires to the outside so sun will keep soil warm

← 3' isle →

NORTH

The frame should be made of rigid material, as string will sag. I use 2"×2"×8'-0" boards, tied together so the poles are not damaged, and can be reused.

To keep the tent from racking, tie a cross stabilizer on each side.

Space horizontal bars one ft. apart on each side.

The Melon Tent works as well for most climbing fruit or vegetables. However, beans climb better if all the poles are vertical.

PEA SUPPORTS

Peas don't grow as high and are bushier than pole beans. A short version of the pole bean supports or caging works well, but I prefer saving the prunings from my fruit trees to stick into the planters for the peas to climb on.

Cool weather crop planters should be used

(Inside out is optional)

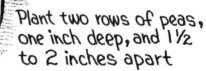

Plant two rows of peas, one inch deep, and 1½ to 2 inches apart

Put four or five prunings between rows.

A higher percentage of my seeds germinate sooner, if I put them in a jar of warm water and set the jar in a warm place overnight.

I have found this to work with all the larger seeds, such as peas, beans, squash etc.

HOW TO MAKE and USE a
POTATO PLANTER

You need two cool weather crop planters.
Do not paint. Planters can be turned
inside out if top planter is slightly smaller
than the bottom planter

Fill one planter
with growing
medium.
Lay 5 seed
potatoes on top.

Cover each potato
with a hand full
of growing medium

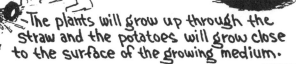

Add second planter.
Fill with
chopped straw.

The plants will grow up through the
straw and the potatoes will grow close
to the surface of the growing medium.

When peas from your garden mature, carefully lift one
side of top planter, reach under and sneak some
potatoes, the plants will never even know they are
missing. Now go in and cook up a mess of creamed
new potatoes an peas.

By using the cold frame for
an early crop, you should be
able to get two crops
a year.

This is not a tire project, but it is such a good idea that I am including it.

How to make PERMANENT WATERPROOF NON FADEABLE LABELS ~

I like to label all my fruit and Vegetable varieties. These are good labels that have been on my trees for years.

Get a board about 4 inches by 8 inches. (measurements not important)

Drill 3/16 inch hole in board

3/16" HOLE

INNER TUBE

3/4"

8"

4"

Tack a piece of inner tube on the board

Get one used ball point pen

Collect several disposable aluminum trays, plates and pans.

With scissors, cut the flat parts into labels, approximately 1 inch to 1½ inches by 4 inches. Fold over twice at one end.

1/8"

Set label on rubber pad and indent information with pen.

Put folded end of label over hole and push pen through label.

McIntosh

Use string or garbage bag twists to attach labels.

PEPPER
Parks GOLDEN SUMMER